THE STICK FAMILY and the FLOOD

Judy Roe Goodman

Gotham Books

30 N Gould St.
Ste. 20820, Sheridan, WY 82801
https://gothambooksinc.com/

Phone: 1 (307) 464-7800

© 2025 *Judy Roe Goodman*. All rights reserved.

No part of this book may be reproduced, stored in a retrieval system, or transmitted by any means without the written permission of the author.

Published by Gotham Books (January 14, 2025)

ISBN: 979-8-3482-6934-0 (H)
ISBN: 979-8-3482-6932-6 (P)
ISBN: 979-8-3482-6933-3 (E)

Because of the dynamic nature of the Internet, any web addresses or links contained in this book may have changed since publication and may no longer be valid.

The views expressed in this work are solely those of the author and do not necessarily reflect the views of the publisher, and the publisher hereby disclaims any responsibility for them.

DEDICATION

I dedicate this book to my loving parents who brought the family through this disaster.
I miss them dearly.

Richard Roe
(1911 – 1994)
Talma Roe
(1917 – 2013)

I also dedicate this book to my sister and brother.

Sue Raulerson
Rick Roe
(1955 – 2010)

Hi, I'm Judy. I am 6 years old. This is my family: my brother Rick, 3 years old; my sister Sue, 22 years old; my mom and my dad. We lived in Columbus, Ohio. We lived in a small house on Hague Avenue, but it seemed so big to me because we had lots of room to play. My grandfather and grandmother lived next door. My grandfather was a carpenter and built our houses.

Sue was a flight attendant with Eastern Airlines and lived in Miami, Florida. She loved her job because she got to fly in big airplanes and take care of the people on their trips. She also got to travel to many cities where she could see all of the wonderful places.

Rick and I were very happy. We played together all of the time. We had a big backyard where our friends came to play. We had snowball fights, played kick ball, tag and many other games. We had lots of fun.

My dad owned a small grocery store on Town Street on the West Side of Columbus. The name of the store was Roe's Grocery. Sue and my mom helped him in the store. It was a friendly neighborhood store where people loved to come to get their groceries and talk to one another.

ROE'S GROCERY

One day it rained and rained and rained. Mom took dad to the store in our car because she needed it. Next to the store was a barber shop. Dad and the barber were scared because they thought the levee that held the Scioto River back might break, so they left in the barber's car. Soon, the levee broke and the water rushed down the street and broke through the windows in their shops. Luckily, they got out just in time.

The barber couldn't drive dad home because the streets were flooded by then, so dad stayed at the barber's house that night. Mom, Rick and I stayed up late because we were very worried about him, but mom told us that he would be fine.

When the water went down, dad went to clean up the store. Mom, Sue, Rick and I went to the store to see what happened and to help dad clean up. There were cans and boxes of food everywhere on the floor. Some of the shelves were leaning. The store was a mess. Dad and mom lost everything. With the help of other family members we cleaned it all up.

Mom and dad were very worried when they lost the store because they didn't know what to do next. However, they didn't lose hope of getting another new store. Rick and I didn't need much and made-up pretend games to play and played with the toys we had. We also had our friends to play with. However, we were sad too.

Some of the labels on the cans of food got wet and came off. Mom brought some of the cans home because the food inside was still good. They were mostly filled with fruits and vegetables. For dinner mom shook the cans without labels to try to guess what was in them. When we opened the cans, we had that for dinner. Sometimes we had funny dinners.

Soon dad got money from the bank and his family helped him too. With the money he was able to buy another store. He called it Roe's IGA. This time it was in a completely different location in Columbus, so it wouldn't get flooded like before.

The whole family was happy again because we had recovered from a horrible disaster. Hopefully, this story gives hope to others who have gone through similar disasters that there is always hope of rebuilding your life.

ABOUT THE BOOK

This book is based on a true story about my family and how we survived the flood in Columbus, Ohio in January of 1959. The flood washed out the family grocery store business and we had to start all over again. The picture is my dad, Richard Roe, owner of Roe's Grocery. He was cleaning out the damaged merchandise from his store. This picture appeared on the front page of the Columbus Evening Dispatch newspaper on January 27, 1959. This story is about a real-life disaster where my family had to overcome a tough time. It shows families, who have faced similar challenges, that they can discover hope, joy and happiness once again.

ABOUT THE AUTHOR

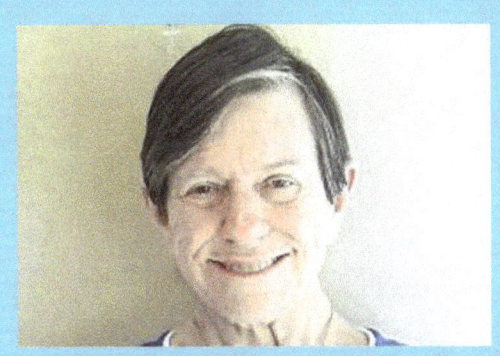

Judy Roe Goodman was born in Columbus, Ohio in 1952. She went to The Ohio State University where she got her master's degree in structural engineering in 1976. She was the first woman to go through the program and graduated at the top of her class. Then she was hired by the Procter & Gamble Company where she was an engineer and operation's manager. She retired after 25 years. Now she resides in West Chester, OH where she enjoys spending time with her children and grandchildren and writing non-fiction children's books.

"I really enjoyed reading Judy's book to my grandchildren. It brings up memories that I tell them while reading it to them." - June

"I loved this book! I didn't know about this flood. This book is a great story about it and how a family got through it! It also talked about how the kids were left to be kids as they should be." - Angela

"I liked reading the book about the Roe family and how you grow up. The book was very good and I can't wait for the next one." - JoAnn

www.ingramcontent.com/pod-product-compliance
Lightning Source LLC
LaVergne TN
LVHW081316060526
838201LV00005B/171